GET PAID!

CASH FLOW CONTROL FOR THE SMALL BUSINESS

Get Paid!

Cash Flow Control for the Small Business

Survive and Thrive in Difficult Times

Alex Hall

© Alex Hall/ Alexandra Publications

All rights reserved world wide
No part of 'Get Paid! Cash Flow Control for the Small Business' may be reproduced or stored by any means without the express permission of Alexandra Publications

Whilst reasonable care is taken to ensure the accuracy of the information in this publication, no responsibility can be accepted for the consequences of any actions based on any opinions, information or advice found in the publication.

Any Business information contained in this publication should not be taken as a substitute for professional advice. It is your own responsibility to comply with all legal, accounting and tax regulations. Please seek advice from your legal and accounting advisors. The author and publisher of this book used their best efforts in producing this book and disclaim liability arising directly or indirectly from the use of the information in this book.

ISBN: 978-1492934691

CONTENTS

Introduction 9
1-Get paid. 15
   Your relationship with money 17
   Remembering to get paid 19
2-Set out your terms 24
   A Business Plan v Terms & Conditions 25
   Keep the cash flowing 31
   Making a business decision. 36
3-Knowing your costs. 41
   Fixed costs 42
   Variable Costs. 44
   Calculating your total costs 45
   Allocating fixed costs 47
   How to set your prices 48
   Is the competition cheaper than you? 50
   Is the competition pricier than you? 50
   Find your niche. 50
4-Varying your prices 52
   Calculating your basic prices 53
   Calculating Variable prices 54
   Producing a Quotation 57
5-Invoicing. 62
   What is an invoice? 63
   Your invoice system 65

- Make time. 68
- Your Credit terms 69
- Pro-forma Invoices. 70
- 6-Controlling Credit 73
  - 100% deposit 74
  - Encouraging settlement of invoices. 75
  - Sending out statements 76
  - Making a telephone call 78
  - Further steps in credit control 80
- 7-When to give up 88
  - Can't pay – won't pay? 89
  - Taking Court Action. 91
- 8-Dealing with suppliers 94
  - Finding suppliers. 95
  - Becoming an importer 99
  - Stock control. 101
- 9-Banking 103
  - Separate your banking. 104
  - Personal & business money 106
  - Read before you sign. 107
- 10- Outside Agencies 109
  - Bookkeeping services. 110
  - Factoring. 111
  - Debt recovery agencies. 113
- Conclusion 116

Introduction

Getting paid is one of the most vital parts of any business.

But for many people it can also be one of the most difficult parts of running a small business.

It can be the issue that makes them cringe, that they put to the back of the mind and the back of the desk.

It's not that the problem is unusual. Many people in all walks of life find it difficult to face their money. They don't check bank statements, utility bills or credit card statements. They don't know what money comes into and out of the household, they just rely on the hole in the wall telling them how much cash is left in the bank account.

That's why so many people slip into the red without noticing, or overspend on their credit card and have to pay the charges for being over the credit

Introduction

limit. It's why so many fear the end of year tax return and put it off as long as possible, even longer than possible and end up paying a fine for submitting the return late, even when they don't actually owe any tax.

Fear of facing money is also why so many people leave their savings in the same account year after year, long after the interest rate has fallen to close to zero and they should have moved it to a new account. Banks make millions – even billions - from people's inability to face the details of their money.

Utility companies make more money because people just let the money be taken from their bank account month after month without checking that it is the right amount or if they could save hundreds by changing to a different tariff or different supplier.

The direct debit system might save some time but it can cost a lot of money when you don't have to bother looking at the actual bills.

All of this is bad enough in your private life – it costs money through lack of potential interest earned and charges you shouldn't have had to pay and bills that are too high.

But when this attitude to money is carried forward to a small business it can quickly become a disaster.

Not checking your personal bank statement can cause problems, not sending out your invoices will cause bankruptcy.

But the sorry fact is that staying on top of invoicing, chasing outstanding accounts, keeping on top of spending and getting the right prices both for purchases and sales – all of these vital processes are often pushed to the back of the 'to-do' list.

And making sure in invoices are paid ends up being one of those jobs that there is always a reason to put off.

After all, you're too busy actually doing the work, running your business, filling the orders, you don't have the time to spend slaving over the paperwork!

For some reason many people even feel embarrassed about discussing money. They feel that they are asking for a favour when they make a telephone call to a customer asking for them to pay account from three months ago.

And the sad truth is that they people sitting on the end of the telephone in those other businesses - especially larger businesses - know that you are embarrassed and uncomfortable in making that call and they will exploit that embarrassment ruthlessly.

Some larger operators even have an unwritten policy of actively intimidating their smaller suppliers to gain cash flow advantages for themselves.

Learning to keep on top of the money is the most important thing you must learn in running any business, so it's a huge problem for the wider economy as well as for the individual that so many entrepreneurs do have this serious difficulty with the area of cash flow control.

But it is the one skill you must learn and implement if you're going to survive.

Getting Paid is quite simply the difference between success and failure in business and an area that I am passionate about.

I absolutely hate seeing a small business being bullied into bankruptcy. I find it totally obscene.

The business of business has always fascinated me. I'm one of those strange creatures who actually

Introduction

enjoys number crunching and spending an evening reading ledgers, and I love to see businesses succeed and grow.

I have been in business, and mentoring start up's and small businesses for over 30 years, specializing in showing people how to make the most of their marketing and how to get to grips with cash flow control, how to give themselves the best chance of success.

And over those years, the area that people have most problems with – and the most serious problems with – is actually getting paid.

They feel that in asking their customers to pay, they're asking for a favour – and some customers are very quick to take advantage of that.

Some business people actually aren't comfortable with dealing with figures and accounts.

Their strengths lie in the actual skills they use to create their business – whether that is painting and decorating, valeting cars, creating magnificent party cakes or gardening. They prefer to just put all the paperwork in a pile for someone else to sort out at some imaginary date in the future while they concentrate on their core skills.

But whatever the problems in dealing with the process of getting paid – they are problems that have to be overcome.

If you don't take care of the cash at the beginning of your business, you won't grow large enough to be able to employ a bookkeeper who'll take care of it for you. Incidentally – no matter how huge your enterprise grows, you should still know what's happening to the money.

Added together as a total, small companies are owed billions and have to wait on average 60 days to be paid for the work that they have done or the goods that they have supplied.

It's estimated that half of all small companies struggle with the problems caused by overdue payments.

Even when they are successful, and they have full order books and plenty of customers, many are still verging on the brink of collapse because of the cash flow problems that overdue payments can cause.

People assume that businesses fail because of the poor economic situation and lack of customers, or simply that they are bad businesses.

But the sad truth is that many otherwise successful small businesses collapse simply because they cannot get the money they are owed.

Money is the life blood of business and bad debts are the cancer that can kill a business if you don't take action.

Understanding this, and setting up an easy to manage credit management system for your business is the route to success, to business growth and the route to being able to sleep at night.

The aim of this book is to guide you through the process of controlling your cash flow.

It's not a book on accounting, bookkeeping systems or teaching you how to read profit and loss forecasts, although they are all useful skills and your might want to invest in a few books or courses that can teach you those skills.

This book is designed to help you face your cash flow problems head on.

Showing you how to take control of getting paid for the work you do rather than letting your customers run your show.

Introduction

It's about showing you how to implement a simple, straightforward plan and then learning how to work with it.

Understanding your business and understanding the importance of cash flow in any business is vital for success and you'll feel much more comfortable once you do learn these vital survival skills.

1-Get paid.

As I've already said, getting paid - or more accurately - not getting paid - is the main reason behind the failure of thousands of small businesses every year.

When a large business fails, employees lose their jobs, shareholders lose money, suppliers lose money, even customers lose money- but when these high street names or multinationals fail, the people at the top normally just move on to another company.

Their reputations might be damaged but normally it doesn't take too long before they are at the top of another company, right back where they were in their protected, comfortable lives.

It's a very different story when a small business fails.

The owners and directors lose not only their jobs, but often their homes and life savings, their pensions and the kids college fund. Sometimes they lose everything, including their reputation and self confidence and therefore their ability to pick themselves up and start again.

I'm not saying this to scare you, but to warn you.

Whenever and why ever this happens, it is always a tragedy.

But it should never happen because you have allowed other people to owe you money.

Don't ever let other people push you into this disaster.

Getting paid should never be an afterthought.

It should never be something you are embarrassed about, and it certainly should never be something you ignore.

It should be at the core of your business.

After all, if you were working for someone else you would expect to get your wages at the end of the week or at the end of the month and you certainly wouldn't let it just go by month after month without getting paid. You just couldn't survive like that and you'd be looking for another job!

Your business needs its money just as much as you need yours. If fact it has an even more urgent need to receive its money because you have to pay other people as well.

Your employees, your suppliers, you have to pay the bank, the landlord, the insurance company, your accountants and lawyers, you have to pay the local taxes and national taxes and you have to be able to pay yourself so that you can pay all those household bills that are still out there and so that you and your family are still able to eat.

The one constant truth about cash flow is that it flows, and even if you don't manage to get it to flow in it most certainly continues to flow out!

Your relationship with money

We have developed a very strange relationship with money. Not just in the way we handle business finance but our own personal finance as well.

In the past it was seen as a strength, almost a moral duty to know exactly how much money you had at any time. Being able to budget was a valued skill and being able to save was a lesson taught to children from a young age.

But everything seemed to change somewhere in the 1980's.

Greed is good.

Buy now pay later.

We entered the world of instant gratification and one of the side effects of this change is that we seem to have completely lost control in our relationship with money.

Sometimes it is almost seen as a weakness to be interested in the details of your money.

A bit miserly if you actually check your bank statements, credit card bills or take notice of the actual amount on the utility bill. After all – who has time to be bothered with the pennies?

I should have become used to it by now, but it still give me shivers every time someone tells me that they don't have the time to check their bank statement.

Well everyone should have time!

If you don't know what's in your bank account how do you know if you're about to go overdrawn or that you'll be refused cash next time you go to the

ATM? If you don't read the details of your credit card bills how will you know if you've been overcharged for something that you bought, if the restaurant bill has been punched in twice or if there are charges that you didn't even authorise.

Everyone should be aware of their own finances.

Of course, the problems are far worse when this attitude drifts into the way you handle your business finance.

There seems to be an idea that demanding payment is a sign of weakness.

'Please Sir, can I have more?'

But you're running a business.

You're running a business that has supplied goods or services to the customer in good faith.

That's your side of the contract.

The customer's side is to pay you for those goods or services. They should pay on time, in full and without any fuss. The fact that they pay the invoice on time is not an act of kindness to your business, it's what they agreed to.

Expecting them to keep to their side of the contract is not a sign of weakness, you are not asking for a favour and it is not acceptable to be kept waiting for payment.

Accepting that this is normal behaviour rather than a sign of weakness, is a first place to start when you want to gain control of the financial side of your business.

A customer is not doing you a good turn by deigning to take your products off your hands, in the same way as you are not doing them a favour by allowing them to purchase from you.

These are the two sides to a business transaction and both sides need to be fulfilled before a successful business transaction takes place.

So, if you do have some problem with the idea of asking for money – get over it right now.

You are not asking for money, you are not asking for them to do you a favour, you are conducting a business transaction which not only includes the passing of goods or services from the supplier to the customer, but also includes the passing of money from one side to the other – from the customer to the supplier.

Remembering to get paid

Although this might sound unreal, unfortunately all too often, it is all too real. People do forget about the process of getting paid.

The people who start and run small businesses are different to the majority in a very important way.

The majority are satisfied to spend their lives as employees. They are more than happy to allow others to worry about getting enough orders, having premises, employing people, keeping financial records, paying taxes, working with accountants, knowing the legal requirements of their industry and all the other things that have to be dealt with when you're running a business.

There are others who want to become their own boss – in theory. But the fact is that it will remain a pipe dream for their whole lives. There will always be some reason why the time isn't right to set out on their own, despite the fact that when the time is finally right they'll be hugely successful because they know so much more than the people they work for!

But the people that do actually take the step are different.

They are entrepreneurs.

Entrepreneurs are the people that drive the world economy.

They create wealth, employ people, buy and sell products and services, create tax revenue, rent premises and grow businesses.

Every business starts with an entrepreneur, whether it's the local corner store or Wal-Mart. Every business starts somewhere.

It starts with one of that special breed of person – the entrepreneur.

They have ideas and they put them into action.

They have plans - and they follow through.

They have dreams – and they chase them.

They take the risk of stepping away from a secure financial world of receiving money in their account every month in the form of wages. They take the risk of stepping into the financial unknown.

The problem is that spending so much time having ideas, making plans and chasing dreams can mean that there isn't much time for the boring mundane things. Things like sending out invoices, getting money in and knowing how much money is in the bank.

Over the years I have met a lot of entrepreneurs who put sending out the invoices or chasing up payments way down their 'to do' list.

They are far too busy doing the things they went into business for in the first place.

They are making furniture, painting people's houses, driving their Big Rig, baking and decorating wonderful cakes, organising events, growing exotic plants or designing magnificent websites.

But actually remembering to send out the invoice when you've done the work is the first, vital stage in getting your money.

For most entrepreneurs, doing paperwork – even if it is all on computers and on-line, it's still paperwork – just doesn't interest them, in fact for many it's the monster in the cupboard, it actually scares them.

So set up a system that will take the terror out of the dreaded paperwork and find a system that will work for you.

There isn't any single system that will work for all types of business, or more importantly, all types of people running a business.

You might be very comfortable with a computer and computer systems and if you are, there are various different off the shelf computer programs that you can choose from. You can also set up your own more basic system with a spreadsheet and word processor.

You might be more comfortable with actually writing in ledgers and using a pad of invoices – and if you are, that is definitely the right choice for you and you shouldn't let anyone talk you out of it.

It's far better to actually send out your handwritten invoices than let the details pile up for weeks or even months because actually turning on the computer program is a chore you normally find reasons to avoid.

You may be a brilliant mechanic, or wonderful chef but even in this switched on, on-line, smartphone world of ours, some people still are not comfortable with technology. If you are one of them, don't panic about it, find a way that works for you.

After all, people have been filling in ledgers by hand and getting their bills paid for hundreds of years.

As I said earlier, this is not a book about account systems – there are many books and websites out there that can help you. This book is about how to take whatever system you have chosen to work with and actually use it to get paid.

So, decide on what you are more comfortable with – or least uncomfortable with - and set up a system.

I have found over the years that setting up a routine helps most people.

If you set yourself a timetable – Wednesday afternoon is for doing the invoices and chasing up unpaid accounts – then you are more likely to stick to that routine. It might be the time of the week that you least look forward to, but it's much harder to ignore an actual appointment with your paperwork than it is to just keep putting it off day after day – I'll do it tomorrow is a very bad routine!

So find a routine that will work for you and stick to it rigidly. It might be difficult at first, but you will create a new habit for yourself.

Although it is commonly said that it only takes 21 days to form a new habit, you shouldn't let yourself feel despondent if you are still struggling on day 22.

More recent research has discovered that it takes at least two to three months for most people to fix a new habit into their life and it can take six months or longer.

Just remember, if you start the process now you'll be a lot closer to your goal in three months than you will be if you keep putting it off.

Your should confront your financial paperwork at least once a week, although a certain time slot once a day will work for some types of business if you produce a large number of smaller value transactions. For instance you might find that your business model means that you should cash up at the end of every working day or that you should send out your invoices in the daily post, while another business model with fewer, larger value orders might only need to send out one or two invoices a week.

But you certainly shouldn't leave it any longer than a weekly appointment with your accounts because you will end up with a larger pile of paperwork and it will be far more daunting to face at the end of the month than if you tackle it in smaller, more manageable chunks.

It will also shorten the period between doing the work and getting paid for it.

Of course there are exceptions.

Some business models are based on invoicing the client monthly for all the work done in the previous month.

If this is the case in your business you should at least keep track of your accounts on a weekly basis so that it is easier to gather the information you need to produce the actual invoice for the end of the month.

Whatever method suits your business and your personal style, you must create a system that will allow you to begin the process of invoicing regularly and efficiently. That is the beginning of the entire cash flow control that any business – no matter the size – absolutely must have to be able to be successful.

2-Set out your terms

When you are setting up your business it's very tempting to just dive in and start.

Some businesses just seem to grow by themselves, from a hobby to doing some work for friends or selling at a market a few times a year until you suddenly realise that you are essentially running a business.

Of course it's always advisable to actual plan a business – doing your market research, investigating the competitors, finding suppliers and checking the various costs of supplies and of course, working out a strong business plan so that you understand what you actually what you want to do, what you want to achieve and how you're going to go about it.

Any website or book that you read about starting a business will tell you that you have to start with a well thought out, well designed and well constructed business plan. You need this to take to the bank or other investors if you are looking for finance for your enterprise.

But in the real world it just doesn't always work like that.

Many new businesses are self financing – that's the best way to start a business if you can, especially when banks aren't that interested in supporting new ideas.

Many new businesses are almost organic in that they grow from the kitchen table to a business unit almost before you've noticed.

And then there's the sad but true fact that many businesses create a wonderful business plan, often with the aid of business start up organisations, but never really think about their terms of business.

The two things are very different.

A Business Plan v Terms & Conditions

A business plan – as the name implies – is a plan.

It details your aims, your strategy for success, the way you plan on running your business, where you intend to be in six months, a year or five years.

It shows that you have thought about your costs of running the business and the sales you intend to make. The number of units you intend to sell and how your business will grow. How much cash will come in and how much it will cost you to produce that income and of course how much profit you intend to make. Profit is very different to turnover. You can turn over millions and still lose money.

A business plan shows that you have taken time to consider what you are doing, what your goals are, what your purpose is in running a business. It can be

Set out your terms

written to show potential investors that you are serious and worth investing in. It can be shown to web-site designers to show them what image you want to project.

It could be a very fancy document with your brand new company name and logo, your company history or your own professional history. It could even have your company mission statement emblazoned proudly across the cover.

And a business plan makes you think about what you actually are planning for your new business and for the changes it will make in your life.

But it still isn't your terms of business.

That is a very different, much less fancy, probably shorter and often overlooked altogether. But it's a very important document, even if it's just a few paragraphs.

Your terms of business are the way you intend to operate business between you and your customer.

Your Terms of Business document is the contract between you and your customer and it is a very important way of focusing your attention on how you are going to run the financial aspects of your business.

Terms of business can be very long complex documents created by teams of lawyers, the small print that we all dread and most of us fail to read when signing a document. But for most business, the basic terms and conditions don't need to be long or complex. In fact it's far better if they are short to the point and clear.

But different types of business require different details in their terms of business contract.

However, whatever your business, the one thing common to all is the absolute necessity of having a well thought out set of terms and conditions. They form the bedrock and the firm foundations of any successful business.

They create an understanding between buyer and seller, between you and your potential customers. If you don't have this document in place there will always be room for uncertainty and misunderstanding between your customer and yourself, and some companies see that as an invitation to delay payment to you.

It's all very well to say your word is your bond, but there's another saying attributed to Samuel Goldwyn, "a verbal contract isn't worth the paper it's written on."

By all means base your business values and reputation on the fact that you are trustworthy and honest and that your word or your handshake is your bond. A reputation for honouring your agreements will help you build a strong name in your industry. But that doesn't mean that it replaces a strong set of terms and conditions and the need to put your quotations and agreements in writing.

Once you are making an agreement with another person or business, you need proof of the details you have agreed in writing. Your terms and conditions are your protection in business.

The one thing that needs to be clear in these documents is what each party - the buyer and the seller - is agreeing to.

The requirements of each type of business will vary but some of the main things you should cover are:
- Setting out your payment terms clearly and what credit period you are offering on your invoices.

- You can also include a specific clause for being able to charge interest on late payments.
- You should state details for any guarantees or warranties that you are offering.
- The timeline for the delivery and for any queries or complaints.
- The timeline for returns – although of course you must comply with the statutory requirements.

If you are selling goods rather than services you will probably want a clause that allows you, the seller, to retain ownership of the goods until payment has been made. This means that if the buyer fails to pay for any reason or becomes insolvent, you have still retained ownership of the goods. Of course actually getting them back is a different matter.

Many types of business can use the same terms of business contract for all their work but there are some types of business where each individual job will require its own specific contract. If this is your business model you can create a basic form of your terms and conditions in your word processing programme. This would have areas for you to add specific items for each different client while maintaining the same basic clauses that can be used for every client.

Of course you might have to create a unique, detailed contract for a larger piece of work, although you should still have a basic map to follow, filling in the specific details as required. For instance, you might be supplying building work or design work where there are specific requirements on both sides. Before taking on a large contract you should know exactly what you are quoting for, what is expected, and when you can expect to receive payment.

So whether you have been in business for a long time or you are about to start your new enterprise, sit down and think seriously about your terms of business.

Either check the contract you already work with, or if you don't have written formal terms of business, make sure it's the next thing on your to-do list.

Once you've decided on your terms of business, make sure your customer knows them.

Any business deal is a contract between the seller, you and the buyer your customer.

It can very simple. The buyer comes into your shop and wants a packet of sweets. They hand over the money, you hand over sweets. They simplest form of credit control - they pay, you supply!

Or it can be very complex contract with payment stages, bonuses for advanced delivery or penalties for delays.

But whatever the terms of the contract are, it is vital that both sides know exactly what is expected from them.

When a business is simple cash on collection like that sweet shop, you don't really need to supply a written copy of your terms and conditions to every customer!

But once you are in the business of sending out invoices you definitely do need to make sure that you have put your terms and conditions in writing to the potential client.

Ideally they will be printed on the back of every quotation you send out or will be printed in your brochure or on your website. It is in your interests to make sure that every customer and every potential customer has easy access to your terms of business – if they choose not to read them, that is up to them.

There are many business models that do not offer credit facilities to their customers.

As more and more businesses have moved online they have also moved to a model of cash with order using systems like PayPal and World Pay where the customer pays before you complete the order.

And this system is not just restricted to the business model where you are selling to the public. Many business to business enterprises also use these methods of online payment with order, especially with new customers, only offering a credit account once they have established a business relationship, if at all.

However, even if you don't offer credit, you should still have a clear and well thought out terms of business document.

You might not have to cover the process of payments and credit terms, but you still have to state clearly what your warranty and guarantees are, what your return policy is and what your terms are if the payment fails.

Of course there are still plenty of business models that will require you to send out invoices and provide credit and it is important to retain control of this credit process.

Having a businesslike set of terms and conditions will tell your customer that you are organised, you are efficient, you are businesslike in running your business. It will indicate to them that you are in control of your credit system and that you are not willing to simply accept whatever terms and conditions they impose on you.

As the supplier - your customer will have precise requirements of you and will expect you to deliver exactly what is agreed, on time and in full.

There are all sorts of laws to ensure that you do supply as expected and described, goods can be refused or returned if you don't. But too many businesses seem to forget that there are requirements on the other side as well.

You expect to be paid.

On time, in full and without having to spend additional time chasing your money.

Being paid should not be an afterthought.

Something that you hope happens without too much delay. Being paid is part of the contract, it is the reason you have supplied the goods or services in the first place.

The principle is the same as that packet of sweets you supply - they pay.

So, you need to set up your systems to take this into account at the very beginning.

The very best time to think about this is when you set up your business in the first place, but any time is better than not at all. So whatever stage your business is at, remember that today it will always be better than next week.

Keep the cash flowing

The very first thing to do in process of keeping the cash flowing, is to realise how important, indeed how vital being paid actually it's.

It should be blindingly obvious. So obvious in fact, that you are asking yourself right now why on earth I'm insulting you by putting the words down on paper – or screen if you're reading the eBook version.

Set out your terms

But the sad truth is that far too many people in business don't see how vital it is. Or at least they don't act on that knowledge.

Whatever your reason for being in business, whether it is the freedom of being your own boss, the chance to do what you want, whether your target is reaching the rich list or wanting to bring your great idea to the public. Whatever your reason, keeping the cash flowing is vital.

Cash is the life blood of business.

A company can run at a loss for a while. For quite a while, in fact, but if the cash stops flowing, you're in trouble, fast.

Look at the banks.

All through the 90s and the early Noughties, they took on more and more risk.

They mortgaged themselves up to the hilt to offer risky mortgages to the public.

They borrowed fantastic sums from each other in a tangled web of deals all around the world. The whole carousel kept turning faster and faster. The overheated cogs were kept going by the magical oil of cash flow.

But once the bank could no longer get access to that seemingly endless line of credit, it all ground to a shuddering ugly halt. One that caused the whole world economy to grind to a halt with it, causing massive pain and trouble to ordinary people all over the world in a mess that is still continuing today.

That is a massive example, on a shudderingly massive scale, but the principle is the same.

A business can often be running at a loss.

It shouldn't be actually insolvent – it's illegal to trade while insolvent in a number of countries, although the legal systems do vary and you should definitely know what the situation is in your home territory. In some countries you can enter an insolvency arrangement to protect the company while you try to make a financial recovery such as Chapter 11 in the USA, while in others you are legally bound to liquidate the company.

But in most countries running at a loss while technically having enough assents to cover your debts is legal and happens to many companies at some point in their history. Just listen to the financial news to hear of the big names who have made a loss at certain times and many of the biggest don't com names consistently report losses but still attract investment.

In general, most new companies don't make a profit in their first few years.

It takes time to build up a new business and there are more costs than income at first. You have to buy stock, arrange premises, pay for printing and advertising. You might have to pay for a website, possibly website design, you might have to employ staff or subcontract some of the tasks you can't complete yourself - you have to spend money.

And of course you haven't earned much yet. Most businesses take a while to build a customer base, so outgoings will almost certainly exceed income at first.

But of course you've prepared for this.

If you set up in a small way, you might keep your own main employment at first, and that means you also keep your main income.

Or you might be investing some money that you have, a windfall or a redundancy payment or savings, you might have an inheritance or have decided to remortgage your home to fund your dream.

And of course many businesses start up with the help of grants or loans from the bank, with the help of a very detailed cash flow forecast of course. Unfortunately, the bank route has become even more difficult in the past few years.

The point is, that although there are no actual profits and not that much cash flow coming from customers, there is still cash flowing from the pot of cash that you set up in the first place.

And this can happen during the life of business as well.

Circumstances can cause a temporary drop in income, businesses can and do make losses at times.

You see this in the biggest of companies when they publish their accounts. It might be caused by specific restructuring, the state of the general economy, specific problems that a company is dealing with, the launch of a new product line or any number of other reasons.

But as long as they can keep the cash flowing, even by increasing their debt levels, they can keep the business going, working towards better times when the trading conditions improve and the business can return to profit.

The common theme is that they can keep going because they can keep the cash flowing.

But if that stops, no matter how sound the basic company accounts, no matter how much profit the books are showing, the business will run into trouble fast.

Frighteningly fast.

Just think of how many things you need actual cash in the bank for.

Wages are the first thing, even if you are the only employee of your business, but certainly if you employ others.

You might be able to delay paying your suppliers for a while - a very short while before they are chasing you for payment and refusing to supply you. But there are other payments that have to be met. Rent, bank payments, lease payments, utilities, tax bills, and cash for your supplies if you deal in cash and carry.

Failing to be able to pay these bills can quickly change a sound, profitable business into a statistic on the failure list as it brings everything tumbling down like a house of cards.

Many large retail companies fail either because they can't meet their tax bills or because their suppliers lose confidence in them and stop deliveries on credit.

No stock, no sales, no business. Bad news travels very fast.

People lose faith in you and once people expect you to fail, you probably will.

Your suppliers will stop supplying you with the goods and services you need, customers will stop placing orders, they will stop buying as they lose confidence in you being able to complete the transaction and it becomes a self-fulfilling prophecy.

So cash flow is king.

No matter what else your business priorities are - put cash flow at the top of your list.

Don't fall into the trap that so many people fall into. Don't be embarrassed about mentioning money that is owed to you or asking to be paid. You're not asking for a favour, expecting to be paid is not a sign of weakness it is a sign of strength.

Don't be bullied into offering more credit than you want to -that is a sign of weakness.

Larger businesses will bully a small supplier into giving the credit terms that they demand, after demanding a reduced price from you in the first place for the pleasure and prestige of allowing them to take your goods or services.

You are not supplying them for the prestige, you are supplying your work to make a profit for your business.

If you do allow them to intimidate you, there really is only one end in sight and once your business has disappeared - causing you all the problems that will follow in your personal life - that large company will simply go on to find someone else to bully and destroy.

A report in the UK by the Federation of Small Businesses at the end of 2014, suggested that almost 20% of small companies has been the victim of bullying by a large customer, while in the USA a report at the same time showed that large companies are stretching their payment times to 120 days in a move that has been described as corporate bullying.

Making a business decision.

It is so tempting to take on that huge contract from a large company.

In one single step your turnover can leap by an enormous amount, and it can be extremely difficult to turn it down.

But - and it's a very big but - you can have a turnover of £10,000 or £100,000, and make money.

Or you can have a turnover of £1 million - which might make you feel great – but you're actually making a loss.

Get Paid

You must always take a long, cold, hard look before you agree to any contract.

If you look in the financial papers, you can always find some horror stories about the way some large companies treat their smaller suppliers.

Now don't get me wrong – I'm not against big business, not at all.

But I am totally against big businesses that use and abuse their smaller suppliers, pushing and pushing to get the lowest price possible, sometimes at impossibly low rates. You have to be able to sustain your business, and in order to do that you have to be able to make a profit.

The big stories at the moment are in the food industry with some of the big names squeezing their suppliers into bankruptcy, leaving them feeling that they have no choice they either submit to outrageous demands or lose the contract. If you have invested your entire production to one customer you are entirely at their mercy.

It can work very successful as long as there is trust and respect on both sides, but you must do your research, work out your figures and think carefully. Don't allow yourself to be blinded by the huge amounts that can be involved in a contact.

There are other potential problems to consider as when you are looking at taking on a contract that will become a considerable percentage of your business. After all, being aware of the potential problems will give you the knowledge you need to avoid them.

So what kind of problems should you consider?

You could find yourself in a position where your main customer will not pay you on time – or at all - which means that even thought you might be making a profit on paper, you're in serious danger of going bankrupt because your cash isn't flowing.

Some huge companies are very supportive of their small suppliers.

They nurture and support start-up businesses and help them to grow, some even have systems to offer grants to start-up companies.

But unfortunately it sometimes feels as if they are the exception rather than the rule and it's always much safer if you consider the potential problems in a new venture or contract, as well as the possibilities.

People might call you a pessimist, but you're just being a realist. Foreseeing the potential problems means that you can take the steps necessary to avoid them.

Always control the cash.

That is the thing it really always boils down to.

Don't be blinded by size and the glory of a huge company as a customer.

Make sure that you remain in control of your cash flow.

Of course it can work, it normally does. Many smaller companies operate as suppliers to a huge company, becoming in effect a sub-contractor where the entire business depends on one giant customer.

Great - but only if they respect you and your company and are interested in a positive working relationship, when you supply what they want and they pay a rate you can live and thrive with.

At this point I have to admit to a personal opinion on this, although you've probably already guessed.

I've always had a problem with the idea of putting all your business eggs in one customer's basket. It gives them far too much control over your business and – when you run a small business – that means that they have control over your whole life.

After all, how are you going to resist if they make an outrageous demand?

Over the years I have witnessed a number of examples where the 'one customer' model has been a huge mistake for a small business.

There have been corporate decisions to move manufacturing out of the UK that left all the UK manufacturers without an outlet for their production.

One large UK department store chain informed their own brand suppliers, that the suppliers would be making a 2.5% contribution the retailer's expansion plans.

Told, not asked – although how could you say no?

This 'contribution' would be taken just before Christmas as a one off discount on all accounts outstanding on a certain date.

So at a stroke, you would lose 2.5% of the invoice for possibly one of the largest and most important orders of your business year.

Many companies depend on the Christmas sales for their very survival and at the very least it is a major part of the business plan for the year, so this would have a major impact on the balance sheet for the entire financial year.

Over the last few years, January has seen more than the traditional sales in the high street, it has seen the failure of a number of very well know names. What hasn't been so visible is the number of unknown names that are brought down with the big companies as their invoices end up in the hands of the liquidators and administrators with very little chance of ever being paid.

And this doesn't only happen after Christmas, it can happen at any time of the year.

Although it's always very tempting to take on a huge order, do always think very carefully and logically about it before you commit your entire business to one large customer. As I've said before, you are basically handing over control of your company to them and losing one of the main reasons that people go into business in the first place. You no longer have control over your own destiny, they do.

If you are an employee of a company they can make you redundant and hopefully you will at least be left with a redundancy payment while you look for another job.

But if your business works for a single company you can lose your entire order book at a single stroke without any financial recompense or cushion to soften the blow.

Personally I would always limit a single customer to no more than 50% of the order book, preferably about 25%.

And this rings true for any business.

If you're supply cakes to the local coffee shop or you're supplying container loads of designer baby clothes to a chain of department stores. Once they take the major part of your business output you are dependent on them and their order for your survival.

3-Knowing your costs.

Although this book is mainly about the absolutely vital skill of getting paid for the work you do, it is also about the wider aspect of cash flow and keeping the cash flowing.

Obviously, getting the money from your customers is central to keeping your cash flowing, but cash flows two ways. You have the cash flowing in from your customers for the work you have done or the goods you have supplied, but you also have the cash flowing out to your suppliers, so you also need to look at your relationship with those suppliers and you have to know your costs of business.

It goes without saying (I hope!) that you know what you charge for your goods or services, although I have known some who seem to just make them up as they go along!

But how did you get that price list in the first place?

Many people just look at the competition and charge less.

But how do you know that they got their prices right in the first place. How do you know what they have chosen as their profit margin, how do you know what their cost base is, and why choose to undercut anyway?

So many businesses have fallen into the trap of thinking that only price sells, that you can only gain custom if you are the cheapest.

Not true, but more on that later.

First of all you need to know what your costs are.

And I do mean all your costs, not just what you actually pay for the goods that you sell on.

The business of selling goods has a slightly different cost base to selling a service but there are some costs that are the same in any business.

Fixed costs

Fixed costs are generally the type of business expenses that are not directly affected by the number of units you are selling, the type of costs that will still have to be paid in a month where sales have fallen.

Wages – even if they are just your wages
Rates and business taxes
Insurance
Utility costs
Telephone and internet
Professional memberships
Equipment
Professional fees (solicitors, accountants etc).

All of these are fixed costs and have to be paid for no matter how many or how few sales you have. You must include the percentage of the total in your cost for each chocolate bar, each minute of time you charge for, each window you wash, each conservatory you build, each wedding cake you supply.

Whatever you sell, your overheads have to be paid for, no matter how low you keep them to start with.

Some are absolutely fixed overheads. They will remain the same no matter how much you sell unless your sales improve so much that you have to move to larger premises for instance. In that case you have to start the calculation again, preferably before you commit to the move.

Some fixed costs can actually vary and they can be altered depending on how much work you are actually doing, for instance your electricity bill will increase if you use your machines more. More staff, higher phone bills. But although in reality not cost is fixed indefinitely, these are the type of costs that you are committed to for a longer period.

This means that fixed costs are a very important part of your overall cash flow.

It can be very easy to be sucked into the excitement of starting a business and far too easy to allow yourself to believe the sales people when they tell you that you absolutely have to have – the latest photocopier, computer system, ultimate mobile phone contract, larger van, 12 month contract for advertising. But all of these 'small' lease payments can add up to a large amount of cash flowing out of your business every month and many of the contracts can commit you to these payments for 36 or even 48 months. So it really is very important to think long and hard before signing on the dotted line and adding to your fixed costs.

Variable Costs.

Variable costs are those that change according to the amount of business that you actually do.

Although part of your utility bill falls into the area of fixed costs – the line rental for the phone, the amount of calls that you actually make will vary over time and some are linked directly to sales, so they fall into variable costs.

In the same way, part of your electricity bill will remain stable regardless of the amount of business you are doing, but the bill will increase dramatically if you have all your commercial ovens working full time or you are using your electric tools twelve hours a day to complete a contract.

Then there are the actual direct costs of your goods, the costs that can be linked to each individual order.

When you're working this out, don't forget to include delivery charges or your cost in time and fuel of going to collect your supplies.

You should also allow for currency charges and of course any taxes you have to pay on the items, especially if your are importing any of your supplies.

Remember, you have to pay for the packaging you use whether you choose to use bags, boxes, bubble wrap, envelopes, gift-wrapping or tissue paper.

If you're supplying a service, you still have costs. Travel costs, vehicles, time, insurance, professional memberships and training, consumables, equipment and tools. They all have to be paid for.

Calculating your total costs

So take some time to sit down with all your invoices, your petty cash, list your cheque stubs, your credit card slips, your bank statements showing on-line payments, in fact everything that is a record of everything you spend on the process of being in business, then you can work out how much it costs you to actually be in business.

And don't forget the cost of borrowing any money. The interest payments are part of your costs.

Of course, you also need to include a figure for your own time.

This is a cost that many people simply don't take into account, they don't build it into their price structure at all

Even if you decide to work without pay at the very beginning of your business, using your time and skills as an investment in the same way as you would invest some actual cash into a start-up, this is not something that you can continue for long, otherwise there is simply no point in being in business.

Moreover, the cost of your time must be built in to your pricing structure from the very beginning, otherwise your prices are not realistic and cannot be sustained.

Work out which of your costs are fixed and which are variable. Once you've scared yourself with how much it actually costs you to just exist in business you can then start to plan your cash flow with a realistic set of figures to guide you. If you do this right at the beginning you can make adjustments to some of the plans you had, for instance you might decide to delay leasing a certain piece of equipment or taking on some fixed commitment.

You can fine tune your costs at almost any stage of your business. Many businesses in the catering industry fail because they haven't costed their portions properly. Cutting a large gateau into eight generous pieces instead of just six oversized pieces can make a very big difference to the profit or loss of a coffee shop if it happens over every luscious cake and gorgeous gateau.

You might choose to trim your costs by redesigning your packaging so that you can use a more economic delivery service or change your manufacturing method to make it more efficient in the use of electricity or raw materials.

The thing is, if you understand your costs you can begin to control that side of your cash flow calculation.

But the fact is that most people who are running small businesses never really look at these costs. They just tend to pay them as the bills come in and worry about it if it is a struggle each month to pay them.

But it is vital that you know and understand these costs because the £20 a month lease on one item and that 'only' five pounds a month on another piece of equipment that you 'just must' have all add up, sometimes to a frightening total.

There are certainly going to be some pieces of equipment and some services that you really can't run your business without and those are the items you will have to find the money for. But there are others that fall into a different category – the things that you'd really like, that you feel you need for your image, but if you think about it with your head rather than your heart you know they can wait for the moment. So let them wait.

Costs can easily get out of hand, even for multinational banks and government departments, so you don't need to feel as if you are a failure if you've allowed your costs to slip out of control. The first stage to controlling costs is to understand them, then you can start working on efficiency savings which very fashionable at the moment.

Allocating fixed costs

Once you've decided what your costs are and which are the fixed that don't change according to your sales and which are the variable, those that are affected by how much you sell, then, you can decide how much of these total costs have to be paid for in each sale.

The amount of the variable cost is quite easy to calculate because you have seen how increased sales affect these costs and you have already worked out the price of each unit.

Working out the percentage of the fixed costs to allocate to each sale takes a little more thought and some realism.

It takes pragmatism because you have to be realistic about the amount of sales you expect to make rather than over optimistic. And when you have decided on a figure – reduce it.

Your breakeven point should be lower than your actual sales.

The breakeven point is the number of sales you have to make to cover your costs, if you fall below that number you will be making a loss, once you go above it you are making a profit.

Obviously, if you sell thousands of small things such as chocolate bars, the percentage of your fixed costs is very small for each individual chocolate bar, whereas if you sell a small number of large things, such as loft conversions, that percentage of your fixed costs added to each individual item will have to be much larger.

But however it is split across however many sales, the costs must be covered if you want to actually make money.

How to set your prices

Once you understand your costs you can be more realistic in setting your prices.

Getting your costs and prices right is absolutely key to controlling your cash flow and your potential profit.

The tried and trusted method that so many small businesses choose of seeing what everyone else charges and selling for less, is definitely not a good plan.

There is absolutely no point in simply undercutting your competitor instead of spending time with your calculator.

How do you know that they have worked out their costs properly? Even if they have, they won't be the same as your costs anyway. Every business has its own unique set of costs.

If they are losing money, you will just lose money faster than they do.

And don't for a moment think that this doesn't happen

A few years ago a very large company - who you think would be run by people who know how to run a business - got into a price war. It's not unusual between large businesses, just look at the supermarkets.

The CEO of one of these companies - who will remain nameless to protect the stupid - actually said, "we can afford to lose more than they can afford to lose"

That is never a good plan.

Actually setting your price to lose money is a very bad idea.

It's a bad idea if you're the head of a huge multinational with the banks and investors and possibly millions in the bank behind you. It's suicidal if you're running a small to medium sized company with your house mortgaged behind you.

In fact, it was suicidal for that large nameless company as well. They disappeared entirely in just a few years after their price war.

Setting your marketing policy as being the cheapest won't get you into a market in any meaningful, long term way unless you have found a way to genuinely cut costs long term.

It's very difficult to raise the prices at a later date and keep customers unless you are a very, very big company and have managed to destroy all potential competitors.

The customers that you do find will be attracted to you because you are cheap and most of them won't stay with you once you try to increase your prices because they were only interested in 'cheap' and will find someone else whos business plan is to undercut you..

A small, even a medium sized company is never big enough to get rid of competition, because even if you did manage to break someone else's business - which is a disgusting business strategy by the way - someone else will come along and you will be in a much weaker financial position to fight off any new competition.

So work out your costs and start from there.

Now you can look at the competition.

Is the competition cheaper than you?

If they are - why?

Do they have a poorer quality product?

Are they a much bigger company than you, so they have economies of scale?

Are they under pricing in which case, they will probably go broke!

Is the competition pricier than you?

Why?

Do they offer better quality in which case, should you raise your standards?

Do they offer better service or does the general market allow for a much higher mark-up than you have included?

Find your niche.

As a small business you cannot supply every potential customer, so it makes sense to concentrate on a niche in your market where you can specialise and charge a premium price.

Take the clothing industry as an example, T-shirts specifically and imagine that you are setting up a shop selling t-shirts.

Who are you competing against?

Obviously when you look around at the vast range of t-shires available to choose from there are some very big differences between them.

There are differences in quality, differences in fabric, differences in quality of manufacturer, differences in design.

But this doesn't totally explain the enormous difference in price between a supermarket T-shirt and a designer label. So choose where in your market you want to position yourself.

You probably can't compete directly with the supermarkets. I'm guessing that you're not the CEO of one of the supermarket chains, but even if you are competing for the same customers - and who isn't nowadays - you can still compete by offering something different in the way that you actually present your product.

Add value by developing a unique selling point.

If it wasn't possible to compete with the might of the supermarket there wouldn't be any independent butchers, farm shops, newsagents or sandwich shops.

So look at your product, look at your costs, look at your market and then decide where to position yourself and use that information as part of the calculation to create your price list.

In the case of t-shirts you might decide to offer a service to personalise them, you could offer a different range of sizes, unusual colours, different designs, better fabric, creating fashion items.

Think about your product and all the different ways you could add variety, write them all down on a large sheet of paper – add anything you can think of, getting as wild and wacky as you like. Then you can sit back and look at the list logically – some of those ideas that seemed totally mad when you wrote them down could actually be adapted a little and used to create something unique.

4-Varying your prices

So now we've had a look at both sides of the cash flow calculation – money in and money out.

Knowing your costs is a vital part of your business decision making, but the other part of the equation is knowing how much you are going to charge.

There are a lot of people running small – and not always so small – businesses out there that have the novel idea that, once you've covered your direct costs for that day, you're making a profit.

It's not that simple!

Running a business is hard work. You'll probably put in more hours than you ever would as an employee. You'll need to develop an enormous range of skills and at one time or other you'll end up doing every single task that your business covers.

But we do it because it can be enormously rewarding in many more ways than just financially rewarding.

The thing is, it has to be financially rewarding otherwise it's not a business, it's a hobby, possibly a very expensive hobby at the end of the day.

Buying an item for £1.00 and selling it for £1.50 does not give you a .50p profit. All the fixed and variable costs have to be met from that .50p.

So setting your prices at the correct level in the first place is vital to your long term success, and indeed, survival.

It is also important to consider the various different prices and discount levels that you will need to be able to build your customer base and to be able to expand into different market. You have to have more than just the single selling price in your main retail market if you want to be able to grow your business beyond just selling to a single retail customer at a time.

Calculating your basic prices

When you are in the process of working out your prices, the aim seems simple enough.

Work out all your costs, divide the fixed costs between the number of sales you think you'll make, add that and other variable costs to the wholesale price you have paid for the item, add your profit margin and – hey presto – you've got your selling price.

You can even create a neat equation and spreadsheet to calculate the prices for you.

Some businesses, especially micro businesses, just need a retail price list.

After all, they will only sell to individual retail customers and they are either not interested in, or don't have the type of product, that makes any other type of price list necessary. It might be the kind of business that involves a great deal of work to create each piece of art and if you are selling direct to your customers that is the price model that you will need.

But of course, if you're going to sell through an agent in a gallery or through a craft outlet you will have to think about the prices that you can afford to sell your pieces to them or the percentage that you can afford to offer them as commission.

Calculating Variable prices

Most business models need to be prepared to offer discounts on their main retail price list.

You need to be prepared and have a discount structure ready for quantity orders, a loyalty scheme or to be able to offer special promotions. Of course you will also need to have prepared a wholesale price list so that you have the information available when you receive an enquiry.

Waiting until you receive that enquiry is far too late.

You have to make your decisions on these prices and discount scales at the beginning of your business planning, rather than panicking when someone is in front of you asking you the question.

If you don't take these potential discounts and wholesale prices into consideration when you are doing your initial calculations, you will set your retail prices too low and will not have left yourself any room for movement. After all – be prepared.

The rates that you want to be able to offer for quantity orders or wholesale orders will directly affect the prices that you set for your main retail list.

For instance, if you have a small sandwich shop you might just price your sandwiches up every day, depending on what fillings and breads you are using that day, although in practice of course, the menu will remain relatively stable from day to day. You probably have a chalkboard or a price list on your counter and then add some specials each day.

But what happens when a company approaches you to do a buffet for one of their meetings or to supply sandwiches every day for their canteen?

You don't have to have a full detailed price list and quotation ready to supply off the top of your head, but you should have the information available in your system to allow you to make that quotation.

And in order to make that quotation, you have to have enough profit margin built into your standard prices to allow you to offer a discount. There's no point in accepting a large wholesale order if it means that you will be selling for less that your cost price.

Although you can take into account the economies of scale that you have when creating a larger order, you still have to have enough profit margin built into your standard prices to allow you to discount, offer an attractive deal to your potential customer and still make money.

It's far too easy to get carried away by the idea of taking a large order and boosting your cashflow, but it's also far too easy to end up losing money on a contract – and that definitely isn't what you want.

You have to know what your breakeven figure is and then never – never – allow anyone to force you below that figure, no matter how tempting it is or how much pressure you are put under.

"X down the road will do it cheaper" is never a good reason to reduce your prices!

A large order that you lose money on is not the sign of growth in your business, it's the way to bankruptcy.

But of course you can afford to accept a smaller profit margin on a larger order, especially a regular order – as long as there is still a worthwhile profit margin. If a large regular order allows you to buy your own supplies in bigger quantities you will be able to negotiate better prices with your own suppliers. A wholesale order may also allow you to increase your production quantities and invest in machinery that will lower your individual item cost.

Economies of scale are one of the ways that a company can grow. It is part of the financial reasoning behind large company mergers and takeovers but it can work for business of any size.

And by the way, if you do run a sandwich shop - why haven't you thought of offering outside catering before, and actually approached companies in your area?

There are many examples where you need to have different prices clearly in your mind.

If you have a website, are you going to offer a promotional discount?

If you have a shop, are you going to have a promotion for regular customers, some type of loyalty scheme?

If you do shows, are you going to have special show prices?

Are you going to offer discounts to members of certain clubs, students, employees of a large company or staff of the NHS?

Once you know how your prices work you will know how much profit margin you have built into them and how much of that can be used as a discount. You may be selling handmade jewellery as individual pieces but you still need to know what you can afford to sell at or how much commission you can afford to pay if and when somebody approaches you for a wholesale price or to sell your work in their shop or gallery.

Producing a Quotation

And then there are the times when you need to produce more formal quotations – and I don't mean a line or two from Shakespeare!

Written quotations protect you as well as the customer and can be extremely useful even in the most seemingly simple contract.

Once you step away from the basic form of supplying goods – here is a sandwich, this is the price – a contract can save you a mountain of trouble in the long run.

It's very nice to think back to a time when your word was your bond, and a handshake was all that was needed, but even thought a verbal contract is still a legally binding contract it can be very difficult to prove what you agreed to if you get into a situation that involves a court.

So don't fall into the trap of thinking that contracts and written quotations are a necessary evil, or even worse an unnecessary evil that you prefer to avoid.

But you have to consider how things can actually change in the real world.

If you are a plumber you might think that you are taking on a simple job to fix a dripping tap until you actually start the job and find that there is far more involved. If you have provided a quotation and have said what your quotation actually includes, you can then go back to your customer and explain that you need to charge a higher price to do the extra work that is required

There is a difference between a quotation or estimate – as the names suggest, they are an estimate of what you think the work will be and how much it will cost – and a contract.

A contract is an agreement of what you will supply and what the customer will pay. It should also include details of when you should supply the goods or services, and most importantly for you, when the customer should pay.

Contracts can be quite simple or long, complex legally written documents. Most contracts are better for being clear, covering the details that are needed without endless paragraphs that no one will read

Too many people running small businesses are scared of paperwork, they'll do anything to avoid it. But getting the paperwork right in the first place makes everything so much easier and quicker in the long run and helps you avoid so many problems.

Computers have made paperwork simple and quick and anyone can master the basics of a computer word processing programme, which gives you enough knowledge to do basic paperwork such as letters and quotations and contracts.

Set up a standard quotation letter for your business, save it as a file and then just fill in the blanks as you need to produce each quotation.

The details of your letter will vary, but you will need to cover what you are going to supply, some trades and business models will also need to state what is not covered in the quotation and of course you need to state what the price will be and how long the quotation is valid for.

The quotation will also make it clear when you expect to be paid.

This might be in full before you carry out the work – for instance catering for a wedding. It could be in stages as the work is carried out – this is a common practice in building work. You might expect payment on completion, and of course you may be offering credit terms to an existing customer – 30 days or end of month following date of invoice are the two most common set of credit terms.

The best way of seeing how and why you should produce quotations and sign a contract is to look at some examples.

For instance, imagine you are running a plumbing business.

A client wants a new bathroom fitted. Great, but before you jump in feet first and rip out the bath, of course you need to know exactly what is involved and what the customer expects. It's far too easy for two people to have completely different ideas of what they have agreed – so although this is extreme, it's just to illustrate a point!

What is included – in your mind and the clients mind?

- A specific bathroom suite?
- What taps and fittings are you including in the quotation?
- Just as important, what is not included in the quotation?
- New tiling?
- New flooring?
- How much would you charge if these will be required as extras?

Does your quotation include VAT? It has to if you are registered for VAT and are dealing with a private client rather than another business.

When will you schedule the job, and how long will it take you to complete it?

Just as important as what is included or not included in the quotation is when and how you expect to be paid.

The very worst scenario is getting to the end of a project and finding your client doesn't have the same expectations as you. So set out clearly in your original quotation and paperwork exactly what your terms of business are.

Do you expect to be paid in instalments as the work goes on, this is quite normal in a large project. Do you expect a deposit before you start, or do you expect to receive a full and final payment on completion of the project or 30 days after you submit an invoice?

All of these things may seem perfectly obvious once you've thought of them. But you have to think of them in the first place, and you have to let your potential client know what you are thinking so that misunderstandings don't turn into disasters.

Once both you and the client know exactly what is being entered into, things should go smoothly.

They are not going to get a bigger bill than they expect and you're not going to have a problem because the job is changing as you get involved. For instance, that the client decides they really want a high end tap fitting rather than the basic one you have included in the quotation. Having it written down and agreed in the first place means that you can have a civilised discussion rather than an argument, and you can update the quotation as you go on if the requirements are altered.

The same model can be used for any business, and don't fall into the trap of being intimidated because your client is a much bigger company than yours.

If they are a good company, they will appreciate that you are professional. If they try to bully you, grit your teeth and walk away, because that is not the beginning of a successful business relationship.

5-Invoicing.

Now that we've dealt with all the different aspects of cash flow in a business, it's time to think about the actual process of getting paid – and that all begins with your invoicing system.

The secret to controlling your cash flow – at least the inflow of cash - is to set up an efficient invoicing system in the first place and to follow through with it.

Sending out your invoice is the first step to getting paid.

Now that might seem totally logical to you, I hope it does, but if you're one of the thousands of entrepreneurs who doesn't actually do this, then sit up and take notice. This will genuinely make all the difference in the world to your business, your stress levels and your life.

If you wait a week or a fortnight before you even produce the invoice for the work you have done or the products you have supplied, you are giving your clients extra free credit.

There's no way that they will – or even can – pay before you send them the invoice to tell them how much you expect from them.

Even if you have already produced a quotation to tell them how much the order will cost, actually sending the invoice is the equivalent of making customers stop and pay at the till before they leave your shop.

There are many – far too many – people running small businesses who can give themselves all sorts of good reasons for putting off sending out the invoices.

They don't have time, they're too busy actually doing the work, meeting customers, preparing quotations, or anything else they can think of.

But the fact of the matter is that, unless you have a business model that is based on some form of cash ay the point of sale – for instance where customers pay cash as they collect your goods or pay you straight away for your service, or you have a website that requires them to check out and pay for the basket before you send it - the invoice is the first step to getting paid.

So send them out quickly.

What is an invoice?

At its most basic, an invoice is a request for payment for goods supplied or services rendered, sometimes a mix of both. A garage will send an invoice for the parts used and the labour charged to fit them.

But there are certain legal requirements that you have to put in place for your invoice system.

Invoicing

These are the requirements for business in the UK and they follow the same basic pattern throughout the world, but please check your local legal requirements for details.
- The word 'Invoice' must be displayed clearly
- Each invoice must have a unique number
- Your company name, address, VAT number if you are registered and contact information must be included
- Your customers company name (if you are delaing with a company) and address
- It must include a clear description of the item you are invoicing for – whether that is a service or goods
- The date you supplied the service or goods
- The date of the invoice
- The amount you are charging
- The VAT amount of applicable
- The total amount (including VAT)

If you are a Registered Limited Company you must also include:
- your company registration number
- the address of the registered office
- the full company name as it appears on the certificate of incorporation
- the business name used in your business
- a geographic address where legal documents can be delivered

Sole traders must also have a geographic address on the invoice for the delivery of legal documents and the traders name or the business name being used must also be included.

Requirements are similar in most countries but you should check with your local authorities for any legal requirements in your business area.

In the USA, States set their own regulations and tax requirements, so you should check your local and federal regulations.

You must also keep your records in good order for the tax authorities. Do check on your local regulations, but the HMRC in the UK and the IRS in the USA require you to keep your records for a minimum of six years. Although as long as you have the space, I always prefer to keep financial records for at least ten years.

Your invoice system

Different types of company need require different levels of invoicing systems.

A lot of the advice you find nowadays focuses on the very latest computer and online based systems and they can make everything much quicker and more streamline, but you need to work with a process that suits your business requirements and you.

Your invoicing system has to be practical and easy for you to use, whether you choose a paper system or a computer system.

Of course most people do use computer systems nowadays and if you have it working properly it will significantly cut down on the amount of time you have to spend preparing invoices.

It will also save you time in other parts of your business and make the financial information much more readily available. It will speed up the preparation for tax returns and give you profit and loss information and many other types of report than can help you see where the financial side of your business is going.

It will also allow you to see what business you are actually doing with different customers, check what their payment schedule is and you will be able to see if the payment time is drifting outside your terms. Many clients start off paying on time or even before time, but then begin to gradually take longer to settle your account. This can be temporary, a deliberate policy or an early sign that all is not well in their own finances and if you know it's happening you can make decisions based on facts.

So a computer account system has many benefits as well as helping you to send out the invoices on time.

But if you choose a computer system that isn't easy to work with or that you find complicated, it won't help you at all. You'll simply end up putting the job off instead of facing the dreaded computer and that is asking for trouble.

If you feel that you have a problem with computerised accounting systems you will actually be better off either getting someone else to tackle the computer or sticking with the old fashioned paper system and actually getting the work done.

If you plan to leave the task of doing your invoices until the weekend, you'll end up leaving them until the end of the month and by then you'll have lost your money for at least a month plus however long it takes your customers to actually settle their account..

If you have a system that you find easy to use then you'll use it every day and send out your invoices on time. After all, if you don't send the invoice, how can you expect your customer to send their payment?

It's vital that you set up your system from the beginning of your business - or as soon as you read this.

However you receive your money – cash, COD (cash on delivery), prepayment or by invoice at the end of the month - having a system that works for you means that you will keep track of your sales and be able to complete your tax return sufficiently.

And of course you'll know who owes you money and how long they are taking to pay, which is a very useful piece of information. It will help you decide if there are some clients that you simply can't afford to deal with.

If you don't have a system to send out invoices once you've provided your goods or services, you might even lose track of the work altogether and forget to invoice for all the work you have done or all the items you have supplied.

And that takes up back to the beginning again - if you don't ask for the money by sending an invoice how will your customer pay you.

You'd be surprised, in fact horrified, at how many small businesses make this very basic and potentially fatal mistake.

Hopefully you'd be surprised and horrified!

So no matter how busy you are with your business, remember that the business of getting paid is vital.

It is not something to put off until tomorrow, or the weekend or the end of the month or when you have time.

Keeping up to date with your invoicing, knowing how much is owed, for how long and when you should expect payment is vital.

Money is the lifeblood of any business.

Make time.

Schedule a regular time for yourself to do your paperwork.

Having a timetable is the best way of actually getting the jobs you really dislike actually done.

If you were employed, you would expect to get your wages when you've done your work and if you're running your own business, you need to set up systems that can bring in regular money in the same way.

The best way to do any paperwork, especially if you don't like it, is by setting up a regular, preferably daily, plan and stick to it.

It does work.

You do get into a pattern, creating a habit that is easy – or at least easier - to stick to, and it means you avoid all the stress of not doing the paperwork regularly. Because although you might persuade yourself that you're too busy and that you're saving time by putting it off – you're not!

It will be at the back of your mind, festering and getting worse day by day, until you spend more time worrying about not doing the paperwork than you would have spent time actually doing it.

And you will forget some of the information, and in the worst case, end up making up some of the details or forgetting about it altogether.

Bad all round!

Not every business needs to send out invoices, but most do. And even that small sandwich shop will need to be able to invoice for a buffet lunch. So you should think about it in advance and prepare an invoice system for the time you will need it, because if you want even the smallest start-up to grow, you will have to be able to invoice a client at some point.

Your Credit terms

Once you do send out an invoice you will also need to include information about when you expect to be paid, so make sure that you state your credit terms clearly.

The most normal terms of business are 30 days, but you can set it at anything you want.

10 days, 21 days, seven days.

Just make sure that your customers know what you expect by making your credit terms clear in the quotation and then on your invoice.

If you are signing a contract with a company you also have to check their terms and conditions of business before you sign on the dotted line.

Some larger companies set their own credit terms for a contract and if you sign you have agreed to them and there's nothing you can do about it.

In fact, you don't even need to sign anything formally, they can send you an email to confirm the work and that means that you will have agreed to their payment terms

You may decide to you will accept 60 days rather than your preferred 30 days, but do you really want to agree to 90 days or even 120 days?

Four months before you can even begin to expect payment for the work you have done is a very long time and means that you are in effect supplying a bank loan to your customer, but without receiving the interest that a bank would demand and unfortunately this is a growing trend.

If an existing customer informs you that they are changing their terms and demanding a longer payment period you should look carefully at your relationship with that company. Do you really want to deal with a bully? Is their business in financial trouble and they are trying to use their suppliers to bail them out?

You have to remember that not all work is actually worth having. Any fool can sell at a loss, you are in business to make a profit.

Pro-forma Invoices

As we've already seen there are a number of different ways that a supplier and customer can interact over payment from the most simple of paying cash at the point of sale to complex contracts with clauses about payment terms, early settlement discount levels and late delivery penalties.

And one of them is the system of pro forma invoicing.

That means that you send a document that looks like an invoice and gives the same information as you will put on the final invoice so that the customer knows what you will be changing if you both decide to go ahead with the contract.

It is actually a request for payment before you supply the goods and serves the same purpose as a quotation.

Although it looks the same as a normal invoice it doesn't include the invoice number and it doesn't go into your accounting system. It's also important to note that it is not a tax invoice, for instance in the UK, a pro-forma invoice is not the same as a VAT invoice and cannot be used as part of your tax return.

Once the pro-forma invoice is paid a numbered, receipted invoice is issued and entered into your accounts.

Although effectively a pro-forma invoice is the same as a quotation it is used in different circumstances, normally when you are much closer to actually proceeding with the order.

A quotation can be quite general in many industries and isn't necessarily expected to turn into an order. For instance you might quote for catering a number of different weddings without actually expecting to get all the work or being able to take all the orders if they come in.

You would issue a pro-forma invoice further along the line of negotiations once you have a genuine expectation of supplying the goods or services but when you require payment before you actually do supply.

It would be the document you send once you have all the items for an order in place but require payment before sending them out. You might be supplying a new client and be unwilling to offer credit on a first order or until they have developed a longer business relationship with you

You can also use them in the case of a special order or personalised items, requiring payment before you actually make the bespoke items.

Some business might never use pro-form invoicing but they can be a major part of the financial system for others and they are worth investigating.

They details are transferred to an official invoice once payment is made and it is that document that is entered into your account system.

If you receive pro-forma invoices you must remember that you cannot use them in your account system or to use in your tax calculations.

If you do decide to include the use of pro-forma invoices in your system always make sure you date them and state clearly how long the offer is valid for. You don't want to be presented with a pro forma invoice that you issued two years and three price rises go!

6-Controlling Credit

You set out your terms of business, made sure that your customer had them in writing before undertaking the work and sent your invoice.

But you haven't been paid.

Unfortunately it is a fact of business life, this does happen. And it happens all too often.

So planning how you are going to deal with this problem is as important as all the rest.

You run a business to make money.

No matter how altruistic you are, no matter how embarrassed you are about asking for money, no matter how English you are about profit being a dirty word - if you don't make money you will go broke!

And making money is when it actually appears in your account.

You haven't made it when you got a full order book. You haven't made it when you've sent out lots of invoices. You've made it when the cash is in the bank.

So plan that credit control.

Don't wait until you have a huge pile of unpaid invoices sitting on your desk and no money in the bank. That kind of cash flow crisis is one of the biggest dangers to any business, especially a small business because you don't have the ability to put pressure on your bankers to extend the credit lines

Even a very small business can and should have a credit department, even if it is run by the same person who runs everything else. And you'd be amazed at how many 'accounts managers' are nothing more than a name on the bottom of the letter.

If it makes you feel more comfortable to be able to say that Mr Jenkins is demanding payment or threatening to charge interest, by all means invent a Mr Jenkins and blame him.

You've set out your terms, so stick to them.

100% deposit

There used to be a joke that you'd see on posters, 'Credit terms – 100% down, nothing to pay!'

But in our modern internet connected world many business can now follow that model and it can help you avoid a great number of problems.

So think seriously about your business and your potential customers and see if you can operate on a cash up front model.

Many businesses as well as most individuals now use credit or debit cards and pay suppliers as they collect the goods they are buying. Cash and Carry has changed from being quite old fashioned and has actually become the modern way to operate, either actually in person or through websites.

It is also much easier for a small business to be able to accept card payments that it used to be.

You used to have to set up a merchant account with a bank or financial institution and they could be quite complex, but now there are a number of different systems such as PayPal, WorldPay and SagePay among others that make the whole process much more simple. If you are in a trade organisation they many also have a package for their members

So don't dismiss the possibility of operating at least some of your work on a cash up front system.

Encouraging settlement of invoices.

There are two ways to 'encourage' swift payment of invoices.

You can either offer a discount for swift payment or charge interest on overdue payments. Of course, you can do both.

The carrot, of a discount for swift payment will encourage some customers to pay early – set it at something like seven days and make sure that you enforce it rigidly, at eight days the account reverts to the full price. You can also set it as a discount for payment with order which means that you don't have to worry about chasing the invoice at all.

This kind of offer will not only encourage early settlement but it will also create a feel good factor with those clients who do settle their invoices in good time. They feel that they are valued and they are being financially rewarded for being good customers. The discount doesn't have to be large, 1% or 2% discounts are the norm.

If you are going to offer this type of carrot it does have to be calculated into your initial prices. If your margins are very tight the discount could take you from profit to loss on some orders.

You also have to have a strong system to stop customers taking the discount when they pay later than the offer time, or even who pay later than your standard credit terms.

You also have to take your tax system into account. In the UK, the VAT regulations changed. Prior to this the VAT was calculated on the discounted amount even when the full amount was paid, from 1st April 2015 this changed and the VAT has to be calculated on the actual amount paid which will mean that the initial invoice for the full amount will have to have a credit note issued for the difference of the amount paid including VAT. This extra paperwork probably means that the practice of early settlement discount will disappear for most businesses.

At the other end of the scale, threatening to charge interest on overdue accounts is one of the easiest and most painless ways of encouraging payment in line with your credit terms.

Sending out statements

Once your credit terms have been exceeded it is normal practice to send out a statement.

A lot of companies don't use these extremely useful reminders and many have stopped using them on the grounds of cutting costs, but they can be a very useful weapon in your armoury of getting paid on time. They are certainly worth the small amount of time and money if it means that you can get the money you are owed into your bank a few weeks earlier than you can without them

You can persuade yourself that you haven't got time, or that it wastes too much in postage and envelopes, but these are just more excuses to avoid paperwork.

A statement – especially when it shows the extra charge of interest on an overdue account – is one of the best ways of prodding a customer into payment. There are companies who won't even think of paying an account until they receive the statement or overdue reminder.

If you have set out interest charges from the very beginning on your invoice, then show this interest as a charge on your statement. You'll be amazed at how many payments of the sum without interest arrive immediately after the statement was received.

And that's fine. The threat of an interest charge has done its job. It's brought in the payment and the fact that you haven't collected the interest doesn't matter. You have payment of the invoice.

In many cases sending out a statement will bring in payment, which is just want you want it to do.

Many countries – including the UK – also have a system of statutory interest payments on late payment of debts which can help you cover some of the costs of late payment and are there to encourage companies to settle their accounts on time rather than taking an unfair amount of time to pay their suppliers.

The ideal situation is that every customer pays on time and you will never have to send out a statement or make a reminder phone call, but in reality if you have a business model that sends out invoices you will also have to send out statements and have a system that is prepared for the times when you will have to send out further follow ups.

Don't be tempted to ever skip on the statement process, it can save you a great deal of time, trouble, frustration and money.

Making a telephone call

Many people who run their own small business will find this the most traumatic process of all the things you can do in credit control.

Actually picking up the phone and reminding someone that they own you money.

But it can be one of the most effective steps in your credit control system and will often lead to the speedy receipt of payment.

The thing you have to keep in mind is that you are not asking for a favour.

It's not as if you're going cap in hand to the bank asking them to increase your overdraft, although you will be if you don't get customers to pay you. You also have to get over any lingering reminders of having to ask you parents for some cash or any other embarrassing or humiliating memory that you are harbouring about asking for money.

In this case you are reminding people that they haven't done what they should have done, they are the ones in the wrong, although you shouldn't go in with all guns blazing. Don't begin the process by attacking the person on the other end of the phone, be calm, professional and reasonable.

One of the things to remember is that many of your customers will have an accounts department and they are almost certainly used to receiving such calls, especially if they operate on a policy of not paying until they have to.

Before you make your call prepare all the information so that you have it in front of you.

You will need the invoice details – number, date and amount and due date.

Prepare yourself to make the calls. It's normally easier if you make all the require calls in one session, then you can get yourself into a routine and work through them all together without getting nervous for each separate one.

The best times to call are between 10 and 12am and then 2 to 4pm. This means that you will avoid the early morning rush, the reply that someone is on their lunch break and the end of the day slump.

I have also found over the years that it is better to avoid Mondays and Fridays.

Try not to rush to the phone to chase invoices when you've just had a supplier chasing you for payment, or when you've spent all morning worrying about how to juggle the next set of payments.

Ideally you should tackle the process of getting money in as a regular part of your business so that you keep your cash flowing smoothly. Your customer owes you the money and should pay you when your credit terms say – so normally after 30 days or at the end of the month following the month you dated the invoice.

This is when your credit control process should swing into action, not when you are facing demands for cash you don't have and decide to chase up the outstanding amounts.

Making these calls when you are stressed, worried or angry will not help at all. You are much more likely to lose your temper, make demands or otherwise ruin your relationship with the customer.

So make it a normal part of your business routine and plan your calls rather than reaching for the phone in panic.

Further steps in credit control

If a statement showing the addition of interest or a rational phone call doesn't bring in payment, you should have a plan that you follow from this point.

You must decide how long you will wait before you start to implement the further stages of your credit control plan.

It might be different with different customers. Some might always take 60 days to pay and you might have decided to accept that after careful consideration, taking into account the amount they spend and whether they pay regularly in the 60 days.

A regular customer, who takes 60 days credit, but pays regularly on the 60 days, is normally still worth keeping as a customer because although you will have to wait longer than you want to, you know when your money is coming in and you can make allowances for it.

On the other hand, some customers might always push you as far as they think they can get away with it.

The answer to this is, don't let them get away with it.

There are companies who almost pride themselves on taking as much time as possible to settle their accounts – and that's wonderful for them, they can use free credit from their suppliers instead of having to pay expensive bank fees and interest. But it's awful for you, because you will have to pay interest changes and overdraft fees instead of having money in the bank, as well as all the problems that can come with persistent late payment.

And then unfortunately, there are other customers might just not pay at all.

There can be a number of different reasons for this. Of course some customers might be in financial difficulties themselves and have trouble paying their accounts.

Some customers just leave payment as long as they possibly can. They even set their terms of payment at 120 days to start with. That's four full months after you issue the invoice before they will even consider settling your account.

If you have agreed to these terms there's not much you can do about it, but if you haven't you should never just hand control of your cash control to someone else, which is what you are doing if you sit back and wait.

Many of these companies simply take as much time as they can get away with, and it's sad but true that it's the folk who make a nuisance of themselves are more like to receive payment, than those who quietly sit back and wait.

So your best plan is to have a plan and to follow it through whenever payment doesn't arrive on time.

- Send out a statement.
- Send out a polite reminder.
- Make a call to the accounts department
- Send out a final demand.
- Send a letter saying you'll be instructing your solicitors.

If will be a matter of choice as to how swiftly you follow through with these different steps.

If you feel that you want to retain a business relationship with a customer, you probably want to keep the whole process friendly and not too threatening.

However, if you are having a serious problem with a customer, you probably aren't interested in keeping the supply lines open and just want to secure payment for the work already completed.

Whatever plan you decide to follow, it is generally more successful if you make these different processes look official. It makes you look serious and therefore they will have to take you seriously. As I said, it's a sad fact that those who demand more, get more and that is definitely the case in credit control.

The supplier who keeps quiet, is far too easy to ignore and very unlikely to be the one who gets payment if there's a problem in the customers company. A company that is having financial difficulties will pay the people who can't be put off and who are making a nuisance of themselves!

So put your full plan in place before, you need it.

Set up your forms and letters so that they are easy to process and send out.

I have included some example letters at the end of this chapter. Feel free to copy them word for word – entering your own information of course – or to use them as a starting point to create your own library of letters ready to use when needed.

If you have to think about what you are going to do when a problem arises, you will put it off and it will become a real problem.

If you have to start to think of your process once you have a pile of unpaid invoices, you will put it off until tomorrow, the weekend, next week, some mythical time when you aren't so busy.

But the fact is that it will fester in your mind causing you stress and becoming an even bigger problem in your imagination and take up even more of your time as you worry about it but don't actually do anything about it.

There's also a chance that you will end up losing a customer that you could have kept, because if they owe you money and the account is now three, four or five months overdue, there's a chance that they will just move onto someone else and you won't get paid at all.

So make your plan and follow it.

In most cases the problem will be solved quickly and easily and if it does go on, you just have to follow through the system that you have set up.

You must always be prepared to stop supplying someone who isn't paying.

I know this sounds obvious, but I've also worked with lots of small business owners who just can't bring themselves to do that.

They are 'scared' of losing their best customer!

Believe me, a customer who doesn't pay is never a good customer. And the more money they owe you, the worse they are.

If they don't settle their invoices for work you have completed or goods you have supplied, they are using your business as a source of free credit. You can't get free credit. In fact borrowing money can cost a fortune.

So work out what you limits are and don't be pushed past them.

Don't keep on supplying your goods or services in the hope that they will pay and the fear that they won't if you cut the supply lines.

If the threat of instructing your solicitors still hasn't worked, you can resort to the Small Claims Court. At the moment (2014), your claim can be up to £10000, and you can represent yourself rather than having to pay a solicitor.

Different States in the USA and provinces in Canada set their own procedures and you should check with your local court systems wherever you operate your business.

You should think clearly about proceeding to court action and you should never do it 'on principal'.

Principals are a very good thing to have, but they can also be expensive, so any further action should have a good financial argument to support it.

As the old saying goes – there's no point throwing good money after bad.

1st reminder

Customers name
Company name
Address

Date

Dear ....

Reference   *(invoice number)*
                 (invoice date)

Our record show that the above account for *(enter amount outstanding)* should have been settled by (date) and is now overdue for payment.

We are sure that this is an oversight and look forward to receiving your payment by *(choose a date about one week ahead)*.

Yours Sincerely

A.N.Other
Credit Manager

2nd reminder

Customers name
Company name
Address

Date

Dear ....

Reference (*invoice number*)
  (*invoice date*)

    Further to our letter of (date of original letter) our records show that your account remains overdue and has now accrued interest charges of (*enter amount*) making the total (*enter total of invoice + interest*).

    We remind you that are terms of business are 30 days from date of invoice (or whatever your credit terms are) and that you have now exceed those terms.

    Please contact us immediately if you need further information or would like to discuss a payment plan. Otherwise we look forward to receiving your payment in full by return.

Yours sincerely

A.N.Other
Credit Manager

Final Notice

Customers name
Company name
Address

Date

Dear ....

FINAL NOTICE
Reference *(invoice number) & (invoice date)*

Our records show that your account is still outstanding and has seriously exceeded our credit terms despite numerous letters and telephone calls.

Unfortunately we now have no alternative but to cease supplying your company until the account is settled in full.

Please ensure payment reaches us by (add date 14 days ahead), otherwise we will have no choice but to forward your account for collection. Please note that further charges will be added to the original amount in this case.

Yours sincerely

A.N. Other
Credit Manager

7-When to give up

Unfortunately, there are some cases, when you simply have to know when to call it a day.

You must learn to be dispassionate about credit control.

Making money in your business is vital, and it must be central to your business plan. But you also have to know when to write off the debt.

Once you've been through your credit control system and if you still haven't received your money, sit back and think seriously before you go any further.

Up to this point the process has cost you your time and some letters and postage and some phone calls as well as the unpaid account.

Anything further than this will begin to add real costs and you have to make a logical decision about the chances of recovering the costs as well as the amount outstanding in the first place.

Can't pay – won't pay?

There are some customers who simply can't pay their account.

They might have a temporary cash flow problem of their own, in which case they probably will pay if you can give them time.

Your long term relationship with a customer can help you decide how you should deal with this. If you have been dealing with them for an extended period without a problem you should be able to gauge whether this is a short term problem that will right itself if you allow them a little time.

Of course, you might also be able to tell that they are entering a much more serious problem of their own – there are normally warning signs. Although it can happen, most companies don't actually fail overnight, it normally takes quite a while for the problem to reach crisis point. So if the problem is just getting worse each month, taking a bit longer to pay you each time, becoming more difficult to get them to talk to you on the phone – it's time to protect your own company rather than risk being dragged down by their problems.

If you are dealing with a new customer – either a company or an individual – you should also make credit checks before you allow them a credit account and ideally you should deal on a cash basis until you develop a business relationship.

Then there are clients who simply won't pay.

There are some who use this as their standard business practice. They find any method possible to avoid paying their legitimate accounts.

If a company concentrates on this method enough, there is always some reason to reject an account, some reason to dispute the total and to delay payment.

They can push a supplier into agreeing a reduction in the account because of some claimed flaw in the product, some failure to agree to the details of the contract or a quality complaint. There are companies who have become rich by failing to pay the full amount for work that has been done or goods that have been supplied.

These are often Goliath companies squashing and destroying much smaller David businesses.

Obviously the best thing is to avoid this problem in the first place. Don't be dazzled by the prospect of dealing with a huge customer, check them out, ask questions in your business groups or on business forums before you commit a huge part of your turnover to a single customer.

If you do find yourself with a customer who 'won't pay' the best form of defence is attack.

They will normally pay the suppliers who make the most noise. If you sit quietly and don't send statements, letters and make phone calls, you won't get paid.

Make a nuisance of yourself, ignore the threats that they won't deal with you again, make regular telephone calls to the accounts department and you are much more likely to be the one who receives payments.

After all, why would you want to keep dealing with someone who doesn't pay their bills? Although in reality you probably will continue to receive orders from them, spend time chasing the account and receiving your money. Customers with this type of credit policy often respect the supplier who doesn't let them get away with it!

Taking Court Action

In the UK you can go through the Small Claims Court system yourself and keep costs low. You can use the small claims system with a solicitor for amounts up to £10000. (correct at 2014).

But if you involve a solicitor or debt collection agency you will be incurring costs.

Even if you represent yourself in the Small Claims Court, you should allow for your time in preparing the claim and appearing at court.

You will also have to pay the court fees. The fees for making a court claim are on a sliding scale and can cost from £25 - £455 to start your claim and if your claim goes to a hearing (2014) .

There would also be further fees if you need to enforce the judgement.

You are allowed to claim interest on the money you are owed. The usual rate is 8%. The rate you are allowed to charge another business in the UK and EU is 'statutory interest', which is 8% plus the Bank of England base rate and if you win your case the other party will probably have to pay your costs.

But of course you still have to be able to get your money from the other party, which can still prove difficult and you might have to add other costs to enforce the judgement and to hand the case over to bailiffs.

At the end of the day, none of this will actually do more than add to your losses if the other company or person does not have the money, if the company goes into liquidation or there is a bankruptcy.

There are some cases, when you will decide to follow this whole legal route and that is perfectly legitimate. You can't keep working for nothing and sometimes you have to go to court to get your money.

But – you must avoid the temptation to chase a debt on principle.

Principals are all well and good, they can be wonderful things to live your life by. Having principals can make you who you are.

They can also cost you a lot of money.

When you know there's really no hope of being paid because the company is about to collapse or when the amount you are owed isn't worth the cost of eventually getting paid, chasing it to the bitter end because of principal is a serious mistake and it can be a very, very expensive mistake.

Court costs, solicitor's fees and possibly barrister's fees in some cases, can add up to thousands in any currency. And when you add your time spent distracted from running your business and the stress it can cause, chasing a principal can be very expensive indeed.

There are times when you should put some things down to experience.

Learn from the mistakes you've made along the way in dealing with this account and make sure that you don't make them again.

Keep in mind the golden rule that should be at the centre of every part of your business and at the heart of every decision you make - no matter what your other reasons you have, one major aim in any business is to make money.

Even a charity has to make money to fund their charitable work. If you don't make money, you are wasting your time, you are not running a business, you have an expensive hobby.

So part of looking after that vital bottom line, is to know when it will cost you more to get paid than you will eventually receive, or indeed the times that you would fail to get anything at all in return for your extra costs and work.

In which case, you are simply throwing good money after bad. Don't!

Learn from the experience, close the file, and move on.

8-Dealing with suppliers

Although the idea of successful cash flow control tends to concentrate on your relationship with your customers, in actual fact how you purchase and your relationship with suppliers is just as important as how you sell and manage your relationship with customers.

They are two sides of the same coin.

How much it costs you to get your stock, your stationery, your supplies, your office machinery and your premises, impacts directly on how much you can sell your product or services for and how much profit you make at the end of the day.

It is an integral part of your cash flow control.

And while it is vital to control the amount of credit that you allow your customers and how long they take to settle their accounts, the other side of the financial scales is balanced by how long and how much credit you have from your suppliers.

Pricing your goods and services correctly is a very important part of your financial management, but it can soon run into trouble if you don't factor in the cost of the money you have tied up in stock.

If you pay your suppliers immediately on purchase, but then have to wait two or three months for your customer to pay for the goods, you are paying financial charges on that gap. And that has to be taken into account in your calculations otherwise you will be losing money without understanding how it is happening.

Finding suppliers

When you set forth to find your suppliers, one of the most important things to realise is that you are in business and to present yourself accordingly.

Far too many people running a small business seem to be almost apologetic that they exist! They approach suppliers as if they are asking for a favour. Believe me, I have actually seen this happen

You must remember that you are running a business, no matter how small you may be if you are a start-up company. You are a business and therefore a business customer.

Set yourself out in a professional way and approach suppliers as if you mean business.

You need to approach a supplier after you have done your research and found some information about them. There's no point in approaching a company that produces specialised packaging for mass market products if you only require a hundred boxes.

Do some research online before you approach a potential supplier. You can also talk to some other business people about the suppliers that they use. Sharing information is one of the benefits of being involved in business groups and other types of networking.

Find out what the minimum order value is for the supplier you are thinking of approaching.

Most business to business and wholesale companies have a minimum order level of some type, if for no other reason than to avoid dealing with the general public.

Some minimum orders levels might be too high for you at the beginning of your business or for items where you only require small amounts, and you need to be realistic about it.

Investing £200 in stock of one type of item might be too much for you, while at the same time £2000 spend on stock of another item isn't any problem at all because you will work your way through a large quantity of the second item quite quickly.

Don't be embarrassed when you are approaching a supplier! After all, if they can't be bothered being polite to you, do you really want to be bothered dealing with them?

But you also have to be realistic, don't insult or make demands. You are all in business and you all have to make a profit.

So, make your approach in an organised, calm and professional way.

Most wholesalers will require proof that you are actually running a business. That's a good thing, you don't want your customers to be able to buy from them at the same price as you can get. You won't be able to make any profit if that is the case.

Wholesale means wholesale – not retail.

They might need to just see a business card, which is the basic item that you should always carry with you at all times. They will possibly require you to apply in writing on your letterhead or by filling in a form on the internet.

Some suppliers need to see invoices from other suppliers and there are some that ask you for your VAT number, although it can still be worth approaching them if you are not yet VAT registered. You have nothing to lose.

Many suppliers will expect you to pay when you place your order at first and then, once you have a proven track record, you can apply to open an account. There are exceptions of course, sometimes, you can apply for an account straight away, and some suppliers such as cash-and-carry - as the name suggests - will always expect you to pay when you make the purchase.

Different models are used in different industries and for different types of business. From a cash flow point of view it's always best if both sides of the transaction - buying and selling - work to the same pattern.

If you sell for cash then paying as you buy your stock keeps things simple. It provides a discipline and should stop you building up excess stock. Obviously there will be time when you want to invest in more stock to prepare for peak sale times, promotions or an expansion in your business.

On the other hand, if your customers pay on a 30 day credit model, it will cause a serious strain on your cash flow if you pay for everything as you buy it, and it will either restrict any expansion plans you have or increase your credit costs as you borrow money to buy your supplies. If this is the pattern you are following remember to include the cost of credit in your costs.

It will also lead to more serious problems if you then have trouble getting your customers to pay you, because the gap between you spending the money and replacing it will grow longer, and the cost of the credit to plug that gap will get more expensive.

This is why it is important to understand and agree exactly what your terms are with your supplier.

How many days credit do they offer if any?

Don't think it's clever to make them wait. Pay on time, rather than waiting for a statement, a reminder or even a final reminder. Always try to maintain a good relationship with your suppliers, then if you do need to ask for something they will be more ready to listen. As with all parts of your business, it is always much better in the long term to try and create and maintain a good working relationship.

When you are looking for new suppliers, don't just rely on companies that are geographically close to you.

There are times where in that makes the most sense, but not always. For instance, if you make regular journeys to your cash and carry for seasonal goods or perishable supplies, you want a supplier that is close so that you can limit the amount of time and travelling expenses that you will have to include in the cost.

But there are other times when using a supplier from further afield may save you a lot of money. In some cases, you will be buying from your original suppliers supplier and that will mean that you are cutting out a whole level of the cost calculation. This is well worth investigating when you a purchasing larger quantities. Of course, the actual number that constitutes a 'larger' quantity will depend on your industry as well as the size of your business.

Read the trade magazines for your industry. Visit the big trade fairs or events related to your industry so you can see how others do things and find new suppliers, new ideas and even new customers.

Becoming an importer

You should also investigate the possibilities of importing your supplies. Buying direct from the Chinese manufacturer or importing from other countries can make a huge difference to your business and the internet has transformed business in this area, making it possible for small companies to work together over thousands of miles.

There are of course some things that you must take into account if you do decide to buy your goods from the other side of the world.

- Make sure that you are dealing with a legitimate business.
- Make sure that you are buying genuine items. As a general rule it's much safer to avoid purchasing any branded items, the risk of buying fake goods is far too high.
- Remember to allow for transport costs and particularly for the taxes you will have to pay on imports. This can increase the cost you thought you were going to pay quite significantly.
- Allow extra time for delivery. Remember that many items are physically 'shipped' in containers on huge cargo ships and they can take a while to arrive. So don't think you can stock up for the Christmas season at the beginning of November. Check with the

supplier, but you should allow weeks not days for delivery.

However, once you take these things into account, there's nothing at all to stop you becoming an importer, and this opens up an entirely new area of business for you. If you have been running a business where you sell direct to the general public, deciding to import directly from the manufacturer means that you can transform your company. Not only can you completely change your cost calculations, you can also make a good profit margin by supplying your goods wholesale rather than just relying on retail and in that case you can increase the amount that you are selling and therefore the size of the orders you can place.

If you are ordering a very small amount, it will probably be sent through normal post and will be relatively fast and relatively inexpensive, but once you want to increase your orders to a worthwhile size you will have to take a different approach to your planning. Shipping can be expensive in relation to the cost of the individual items, which means that it's far more effective to place a smaller number of larger orders a year.

Although air freight can look more expensive than shipping by sea, it is faster and you normally have a better idea of the additional costs. The extra costs of sea freight can really add up with dock charges, storage, port fees and clearance fees all being added to your initial invoice costs.

Importing is definitely an interesting area and can completely transform your business as well as your cash flow, so it is worth investigating if you can see how it could work with your own personal business requirements.

Stock control.

Obviously, most businesses will carry stock and that does mean keeping your cash tied up in the stock room, but you should have a clear picture of the details before you go on some mad spending spree.

You must know how much money you are committing to stock and how long you will realistically carry it in stock for before you can turn it back into money.

When you are thinking of investing a larger sum of money in order to qualify for a larger discount from your supplier, you need to know whether the saving you will make per item by investing more money upfront is worth the cost of having to keep your money locked up in that item for longer. If you can lower your price and sell much more stock much faster, than the investment is worthwhile. On the other hand you might be dealing with a product where you can keep the price up and it might be worth making the investment with a much longer turnaround but much higher profit margin in mind. Traditionally, a high end jeweller might take a number of years to sell a piece but the profit margin means that it is still profitable.

Having an efficient stock control system is a vital part of controlling your overall cash flow.

It is far too easy to buy too much stock simply because you not know what stock you already have. If you don't know what is in the stock room or where in the stockroom it actually is you are much more likely to just go and buy more when an order comes in and that is a total waste of money.

Stocktaking isn't just a boring waste of time that has to be done at the end of the financial year.

Stock taking is a vital process of finding exactly what you actually have sitting on the shelves, how long it has been there and what condition it is in.

It's also a way of seeing how much of your capital you have tied up in stock and what your stock turnover you have.

Knowing what items sell fast and which don't sell at all are equally important.

If you have items that sell fast you could improve your cashflow by buying in larger quantities which will save on delivery and transport costs and could allow you to negotiate better quantity discounts.

At the other end of the scale, discovering which items just sit on the shelf – and don't worry, we've all made the mistake of buying items that just don't sell – will give you the chance to decide how you are going to release the cash tied up in that stock.

Making even the smallest profit is better than keeping items in the stockroom. Eventually you will end up getting rid of them anyway because they are damaged or just go completely out of fashion.

It's much better to have a clearance event and turn your sluggish stock back into money that can move back into your cashflow.

You might even think of some way of packaging them or using the parts to make a product that will be a success.

9-Banking

"I have always been afraid of banks."
Andrew Jackson, seventh president,
United States of America.

There's an old joke in the business world,
Owe the bank £1000, and you have a problem - Owe the bank £1 million pounds, and they have a problem.

The banking world has been turned upside down over the last few years and has shown the whole world is that, far from being all knowing financial gods, they actually have feet of clay, and some people in the banking industry are just downright dishonest.

But even now, many business people, especially those running small businesses, still act as if the bank is all-powerful and all-knowing.

The banks sell the image that they are there to help and support business, providing the small business owner with help and advice, being there for you in tough times.

Far too many business owners have found out just how false that is, especially in recent years.

In order to protect yourself financially, you must learn, early on in your business career, that banks are just another type of business.

The companies that they look out for and support are themselves and you should bear that in mind when you organise your banking.

Separate your banking.

Every bank organisation will do their very best to convince you that you have to put all your financial dealings through one institution – theirs of course!

I was lucky enough at the very beginning of my business career many years ago, to be given advice by the founder and chief executive of a very large publicly listed company. Right from the first days of his business, he had accounts with as many banks as possible. Any one of them would have loved to have had his entire banking business, but he made sure that he was in control of his company and then his group of companies, rather than some banker.

He advised me to follow the same route. Divide the business between different banks and make sure that you stay in control of the money.

I have always followed his advice and there have been times when the outside financial market has caused me to be very grateful that I did.

It is always good advice in business not to put all your eggs in one basket, whether that's relying on one bank, one large customer or one large supplier. But that is exactly what most people do when it comes to control of their money.

Every company, no matter what size or how successful has ebbs and flows in their business, times when they have money to spare and times when cash is a bit tighter or when they needed injection of cash for expansion.

It's when you owe money to the bank that you are most vulnerable.

As many companies have discovered, especially in recent years, your business can be put in serious jeopardy because of the actions of a bank.

Through no fault of your own you can find your overdraft facility reduced or withdrawn altogether with very little notice due to the situation in the wider financial market.

You have no guarantee that your supply of money is secure even if you are following the terms that have been set out. And if your bank moves the goalposts without warning because of their own internal problems, you will be plunged into an instant cash flow crisis.

And it will be the very worst type of cash flow crisis, because the money that you receive from your customers just disappears into the black hole of your bank account. Your customers are paying you, but it is the bank that is receiving the money. This equals disaster.

But if you have accounts in more than one bank, you can choose where to put the money you receive and keep your cash flowing. Control stays with you.

Never hand over control of your money to someone else.

It may take a little more work on your behalf keeping track of where your money is, having automatic payments directed into different bank accounts or having more than one account setup on an electronic payment system, but it is worth the extra time.

Although it is an extreme example, and one that hopefully will never be seen in Europe again, people and businesses in Cyprus have discovered just how devastating it can be to rely on a single bank.

When Laiki, the bank at the centre of the financial crisis in Cyprus went bankrupt, people lost thousands of euros from their accounts in an automatic levy on deposits over 100,000 euros held with the bank and the whole banking system was plunged into crisis.

People were unable to draw cash from their accounts and businesses were starved of cash as well as losing significant amounts of their capital. I admit this was a very extreme example in the middle of a serious financial crisis, but a bit of paranoia in business can be useful, it can help you avoid the worst disasters.

Personal & business money

If nothing else, you should always use a different bank for your business and personal accounts, keeping your own personal money ring fenced from your business unless you decide to use it.

The bank might not actually be able to move your money from one account to another without your permission, but they can certainly make it impossible for you to refuse a request.

If this happens, your safety net of money held on deposit suddenly disappears, taking with it your future plans for your business, your expansion plans or even the plans for your personal future.

The whole purpose of this book is to show you how to say in control of the cash flow of your business and if things go wrong with something in the banking system, the very place that you hold your cash for safety can become the biggest danger to it.

Another piece of advice that the banking system regularly promotes is that you should almost look upon your bank as a kindly supporter, feeling that you can go to them for advice in times of need. But think carefully before pouring out your woes to the bank manager - if you can find one - or to the account manager who changes every few months if you're lucky and sometimes in every phone call.

The main business of a bank is to protect the bank. If they think that their money might be at risk, their first action will be to protect themselves. Not your business or your personal finances.

That could mean reducing your overdraft or making you sign more personal guarantees, but never fall into the trap of thinking that they are like a helpful benevolent uncle. They are not. There is a very good argument for thinking that the less they know, the less they will worry you!

Read before you sign.

Finally, always read every word of an agreement before you sign it.

So many people seem to think that they haven't got time to waste reading the small print – and it can be very small.

But if you don't read it, and I mean read it carefully and understand every word, how do you know what you're agreeing to?

Finding out when you receive a demand you were never expecting or when the interest rate is increased without warning, or you have an unexpected charge for the set up fee, is too late.

There's no point complaining that the fee is unfair, the interest hike too severe or the change of overdraft limit has caused a serious cash flow problem. If you signed the agreement, you agreed.

Read everything before you sign. The applies to any agreement, any legal document, contracts are legally binding agreements whether you are signing a loan agreement at your bank, the papers to open a new account, a credit card agreement, the rental agreement for your premises or for a new photocopier.

Never add your signature to anything you haven't read and understood properly.

10- Outside Agencies

There are a number of different services that you can use to help you keep control of the financial side of your business, taking the day to day maintenance of your credit control system off your desk.

If you really struggle with the financial side of your business this can be a worthwhile investment, swapping some of your money in return for giving you more time to concentrate on the things that you are good at.

It is far better to pay someone else to do the work in a few hours, rather than spending days, and sleepless nights trying to do it yourself.

If you really struggle with the financial control of your business you will be holding back your potential success by focusing on what you can't do, rather than on what you can do really well.

There are a number of different ways that you can approach this problem.

Bookkeeping services.

You can decide to actually employ someone to do the work, a bookkeeper or someone from your accountant's office.

You will probably only need to buy a few hours a week rather than having to employ someone full time. After all, sending out your invoices to customers once a week is better than only doing them once a month!

There are companies and individuals who offer bookkeeping services and they will be able to take care of a range of your financial work, depending on what you decide you need help with.

Your purchase accounting as well as sales accounting and credit control, making sure your tax records and returns are in order, preparing your nominal ledger and dealing with cash and banking. They can even manage your payroll if you need help with that.

Many people confuse bookkeeping and accountancy services, but there is a difference.

Accountants look at the bigger picture, preparing reports and accounts and giving advice on the overall business. They will sometimes help you set up your systems and put in place the methods that you will use for the day to day recording of transactions.

Bookkeepers deal with those day to day transactions of the business and will take that headache away from you. A good bookkeeper will help to keep you sane if you are one of the thousands who struggle with the financial paperwork of running a business.

Your invoices will be sent out on time, credit control will be taken care of, your purchase invoices will be paid on time keeping your lines of supply moving smoothly.

You will also be able to see what profit or loss you are making, how much cash you have in the bank and how much money you are owed. You can use this information to decide what parts of your business are worth expanding and what customers or products you should say goodbye to.

This is the type of cash control that every business, large or small, must have to survive. If you really can't manage to stay on top of it yourself then you should pay someone else who can do it for you. It can save you thousands, it can save you stress and it can save your business.

Factoring.

Factoring is a service that many banks and financial institutions worldwide offer as one of their services, sometimes through another organisation or partner companies.

It is a service that is generally used by smaller businesses who want to avoid the problems caused by failing to get their invoices paid on time, which of course causes problems with cash flow.

It is also a service that tends to become more fashionable in times of economic downturn, mainly because it becomes more difficult to raise money from the banks through normal lending and bank overdrafts.

The basic idea of factoring is that you hand over your invoices to this other company and most services pay you 85-90% of the value up front - on a monthly basis.

This means that you don't have to wait months for payment, you know when your money will arrive and you don't have to spend hours on credit control chasing up unpaid invoices and sending out statements.

Once your customer pays the invoice, the factoring service will send you the balance on your next payment less the fees for service, which can vary between 0.5% and 5%. You will also pay a charge similar to that on a bank overdraft on the money that has been advanced

And you do have to take that into account.

Factoring isn't free, there are various fees to take into account.

There are normally set up fees, possibly legal fees and a service charge on the invoices and the fee that replaced the amount you would pay on a straightforward bank overdraft. So you must read all the information before you decide to use a factoring service and before you choose which one you want to use. They can have a severe affect on your profit figures depending on what your profit margin is in the first place.

Many factoring services also require a minimum turnover which could fifty thousand or two hundred and fifty thousand, although there are some companies who offer the service from start-up.

You can also choose between recourse factoring and non-recourse factoring services.

If you choose recourse factoring you still hold the risk of any bad debts. Normally if an invoice isn't paid after 120 days (this can vary) it will bounce back onto your desk and the money advanced on it will come off your next payment.

Non-recourse factoring will protect you from this risk of bad debts, but of course it will cost you a higher percentage on your entire turnover.

In turning over your invoicing to another company you will rid yourself of the headaches of dealing with this part of the business and you will improve your cash-flow, but you will also lose control of how your customers are treated in this part of the transaction and it will cost you money.

It can also take time to actually end a factoring agreement - months rather than weeks. So it isn't something you should rush into without some serious thought and some serious work with your calculator.

Debt recovery agencies.

You may have a system in place that makes most of your credit control system a very smooth operation.

You send out your invoices on time and follow up with statements. You understand who owes you money, how long they have owed it for and when you can expect payment.

But even the most organised businesses can have a problem when a customer doesn't pay. It can be uncomfortable to chase your customers, and – a point we started this book with - many people are just embarrassed to chase money.

Chasing debt can be stressful, time consuming and frustrating and there are times when it is far better to hand the whole process over to a debt collection agency who will deal with the process efficiently and professionally.

Outside Agencies

Not a thug with a bat and an obviously broken nose - a professional, trustworthy debt collection agency.

Many people are uncomfortable about the idea of using a debt collection agency, but it can be a quick and easy way to recover outstanding amounts and it is less confrontational than having to chase customers repeatedly yourself, which can lead to alienating the customer.

Although there are large agencies who either work for banks or utility companies chasing debts from customers that have already been written off, there are other specialist companies who work with smaller client companies and they tend to offer a much more personalised service, they also are more likely to recognise the importance of protecting your brand and your reputation for customer care.

There are clients who simply have a policy of not paying their accounts until they absolutely have to. This is the way they operate their business and so they do not take it personally if you have to resort to threats of court actions and letters from a solicitor or debt collection agency.

An agency will take over the process once you have reached your limit – which for many people is after sending out the invoice or at most a single statement or phone call.

This is because most people running a small business simply don't know where to go from there if the statement hasn't brought the payment in.

An agency will have a range of carefully crafted letters that are designed to encourage a swift response. If it doesn't, they also have staff that can make the phone calls that so many people find impossible to manage.

This process of gentle, professional pushing will more often than not result in the payment of the account and everything will continue as normal. Some clients will always require this process as part of the credit control of their account, for others it the non-payment will have been caused by some temporary problem or oversight. Of course there are other customers who will take your account more seriously in future once they discover that you are not one of the suppliers who can be put off endlessly.

Obviously if you are dealing with a client who owes money for a significant amount of time and where you have attempted to obtain payment yourself before handing it over to an agency, you do risk any future business relationship you may have with that particular customer.

But if it has reached the stage where you have to seriously chase the debt, the relationship has soured anyway and you probably don't want to deal with them again if they won't or can't pay.

This also relates to chapter seven. There are times when it just isn't worth throwing good money after bad.

If you are faced with a customer – either a person or another business – who simply 'cannot' pay, you have to decide whether it is really worth pushing them. You could be adding to your own costs with absolutely no chance of recovering anything if they go into liquidation or file for bankruptcy. If you think that there is a chance that they will pay, that they actually want to pay, it is probably worth considering allowing them to set up a payment schedule to clear the amount in instalments.

Conclusion

Managing your cash flow successful is central to running your business successfully.

Obviously it is not the entire picture, you also have to be able to find customers for your service or products. You have to have good supply lines, successful marketing and good customer service.

And of course you have to be able to get customers in the first place.

But once you have all the other building blocks in place, the whole thing can come tumbling down if you don't have successful cash flow systems in place.

Hopefully by now you can see how all the different pieces fit together, both how you invest your money as well as being able to get the money in once you have done the work or supplied the goods.

Whatever business model you choose, having the right systems in place to allow you to keep control of your cash flow and to understand exactly where it is flowing and where it might be getting stuck when it isn't flowing, will help you run your business and your life smoothly and with much less stress – and less stress is always a good thing in business.

www.ingramcontent.com/pod-product-compliance
Lightning Source LLC
Chambersburg PA
CBHW051218170526
45166CB00005B/1944